HISTORY UNDER COVER

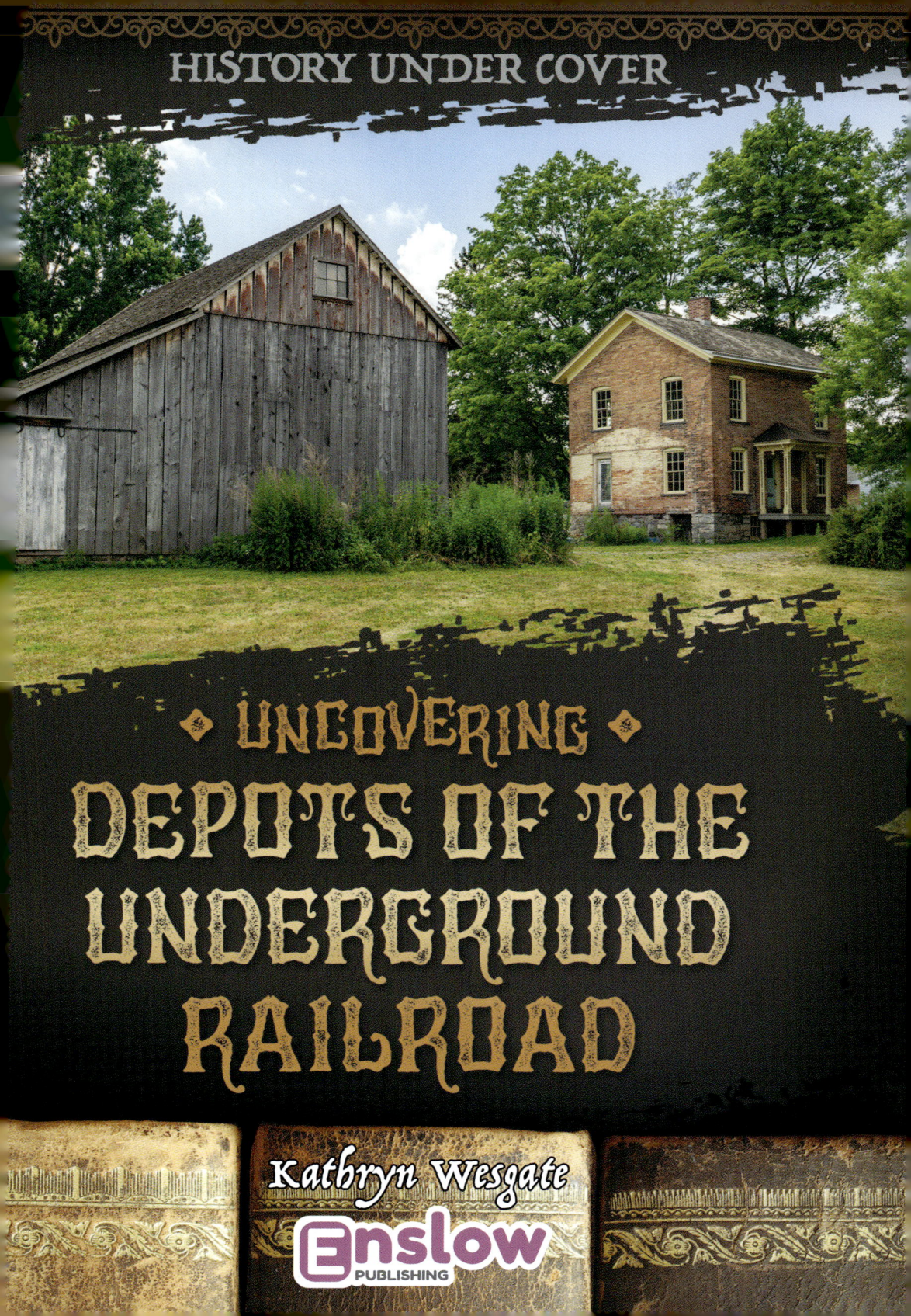

UNCOVERING

DEPOTS OF THE UNDERGROUND RAILROAD

Kathryn Wesgate

Enslow
PUBLISHING

Please visit our website, www.enslow.com. For a free color catalog of all our high-quality books, call toll free 1-800-398-2504 or fax 1-877-980-4454.

Cataloging-in-Publication Data

Names: Wesgate, Kathryn.
Title: Uncovering depots of the Underground Railroad / Kathryn Wesgate.
Description: New York : Enslow Publishing, 2023. | Series: History under cover | Includes glossary and index.
Identifiers: ISBN 9781978528789 (pbk.) | ISBN 9781978528802 (library bound) | ISBN 9781978528796 (6pack) | ISBN 9781978528819 (ebook)
Subjects: LCSH: Underground Railroad–Juvenile literature. | Fugitive slaves–United States–History–19th century--Juvenile literature.
Classification: LCC E450.W4226 2023 | DDC 973.7'115–dc23

Published in 2023 by
Enslow Publishing
29 East 21st Street
New York, NY 10010

Portions of this work were originally authored by Caroline Kennon and published as *Depots of the Underground Railroad*. All new material this edition authored by Kathryn Wesgate.

Designer: Leslie Taylor
Editor: Kate Mikoley

Photo credits: Cover, p. 8 Zack Frank/Shutterstock.com; series art (scrolls) Magenta10/Shutterstock.com; series art (back cover leather texture) levan828/Shutterstock.com; series art (front cover books) RMMPPhotography/Shutterstock.com; series art (title font) MagicPics/Shutterstock.com; series art (ripped inside pgs) kaczor58/Shutterstock.com; p. 4 North Wind Picture Archives/Alamy.com; p. 5 Courtesy of the Metropolitan Museum of Art, New York; p. 6 Everett Collection/BridgemanImages.com; p. 7 Heidi Besen/Shutterstock.com; p. 9 https://commons.wikimedia.org/wiki/File:Undergroundrailroadsmall2.jpg; p. 10 Associated Press/APimages.com; p. 11 (bottom) North Wind Picture Archives/Alamy.com; p. 11 (top) Everett Collection/Shutterstock.com; p. 12 https://commons.wikimedia.org/wiki/File:Harriet_Tubman_Civil_War_Woodcut.jpg; p. 13 (left) Everett Collection/Shutterstock.com; p. 13 (right) https://commons.wikimedia.org/wiki/File:Harriet_Tubman_late_in_life.jpg; p. 14 Chronicle/Alamy.com; p. 15 Everett Collection/Shutterstock.com; p. 16 karenfoleyphotography/Shutterstock.com; p. 17 Charles Phelps Cushing/Alamy.com; p. 18 https://commons.wikimedia.org/wiki/File:The_Dr._Nathan_M._Thomas_House.jpg; p. 19 BD Images/Shutterstock.com; p. 20 Associated Press/APimages.com; p. 21 ttps://commons.wikimedia.org/wiki/File:Lewelling_Salem_IA.JPG; p. 22 https://commons.wikimedia.org/wiki/File:Milton_House_Milton_Wisconsin_October_2011.jpg; p. 23 (left) Randy Duchaine/Alamy.com; p. 23 (right) Randy Duchaine/Alamy.com; p. 24 Historic Images/Alamy.com; p. 25 (bottom) Everett Collection/Shutterstock.com; p. 25 (top) https://commons.wikimedia.org/wiki/File:Gerrit_Smith_house,_Peterboro,_New_York.jpg; p. 26 Frederick Douglass, head-and-shoulders portrait, facing left., [Between 1870 and 1900] Photograph/loc.gov; p. 27 Cindy Hopkins/Alamy.com; p. 29 Everett Collection/Shutterstock.com; p. 29 Auchara Phuangsitthi/Shutterstock.com.

Printed in the United States of America

Some of the images in this book illustrate individuals who are models. The depictions do not imply actual situations or events.

CPSIA compliance information: Batch #CSENS23: For further information, contact Enslow Publishing, New York, New York, at 1-800-398-2504.

Find us on

Contents

Words in the glossary appear in bold or highlighted type the first time they are used in the text.

The Railroad That Wasn't a Railroad

By the mid-1800s, newspapers in New York City, Boston, Massachusetts, and other American cities were using the term "Underground Railroad" to describe how some enslaved people mysteriously escaped their enslavers. Several stories exist for how the term came about. One says it happened in 1831, when an enslaved Kentucky man named Tice Davids swam across the Ohio River toward freedom. According to the story, Davids's enslaver said he must have "gone off on an underground railroad." Other stories tell of enslaved people discussing an "underground railroad to Boston."

Of course, the Underground Railroad wasn't an actual railroad. It was a massive effort by enslaved and free people alike to secretly bring thousands of enslaved people to freedom in the North. For many, the final destination was Canada, often called the "Promised Land."

Artists often used real experiences of people on the Underground Railroad to shape their work. This piece shows a man escaping slavery by crossing the Ohio River, like Tice Davids may have done.

This painting is by Theodor Kaufmann, a soldier who fought for the North in the American Civil War. Some art experts think this work shows the lack of a clear route to liberty for enslaved people trying to escape.

~ Who Ran the Railroad? ~

Some say that an organized system to help people escape enslavement may have begun as early as the end of the 18th century. In 1786, George Washington complained that one of the people he enslaved had run away with help from a "society of Quakers, formed for such purposes." The Quakers were a religious group who were strongly and publicly against slavery. In the 1800s, the Quakers were a major part of the Underground Railroad. However, it was free Northern Black Americans who were the main force in running the Underground Railroad.

Looking for Freedom

In the 18th and 19th centuries, enslavement was common in America. Those enslaved were mostly descendants of Africans. After the American Revolution, northern states such as Pennsylvania and New York began to abolish, or end, slavery. Southern states such as Alabama and Mississippi retained it. The economy in the South largely depended on the forced labor of enslaved people.

Wanting freedom, many enslaved people in the South attempted to escape north. They often required help getting there. This help took the shape of a hidden network of people and places leading to freedom. As the term "Underground Railroad" became popular for the network, so did other terms relating to trains. "Conductors," "passengers," and "stations" were all used to describe the individuals and locations in the Underground Railroad. Secret codes helped get people to freedom.

The conductor was responsible for moving those on the run from one depot, or station, to the next. Harriet Tubman was one of the most famous conductors.

Today, statues all over the country honor the important work Harriet Tubman and many others did on the Underground Railroad. This one is in Boston, Massachusetts.

~ Enslavement in the North ~

History books often make it seem as though slavery was only an issue in the South. While Northern states did end slavery before the South, it's important to note that slavery existed throughout America. In many states, even after laws were passed to free enslaved people, the practice remained for a time. For example, New York passed an **emancipation** law in 1799, but many enslaved people in the state weren't officially freed until 1827. **Census** records even show that some were still enslaved until at least 1830.

On the Underground Railroad, depots and stations were the homes and businesses where those escaping enslavement would stop to hide, sleep, and eat. Those who owned these locations and welcomed escapees were called stationmasters. Individuals who contributed money or supplies were called stockholders.

The Harriet Tubman National Historical Park in Auburn, New York, lets visitors see where Tubman lived for a time.

A majority of the individuals helping to get people to freedom were Black. Most of the people involved only knew of the local efforts to help people escape slavery and not of the overall operation. The Underground Railroad succeeded because of the hard work of these individual people at the local level, not necessarily because of a larger system of routes.

Only a few thousand enslaved people escaped each year. However, enslavers considered these people to be their stolen property. Escapees—and those who helped them—became a big concern for enslavers.

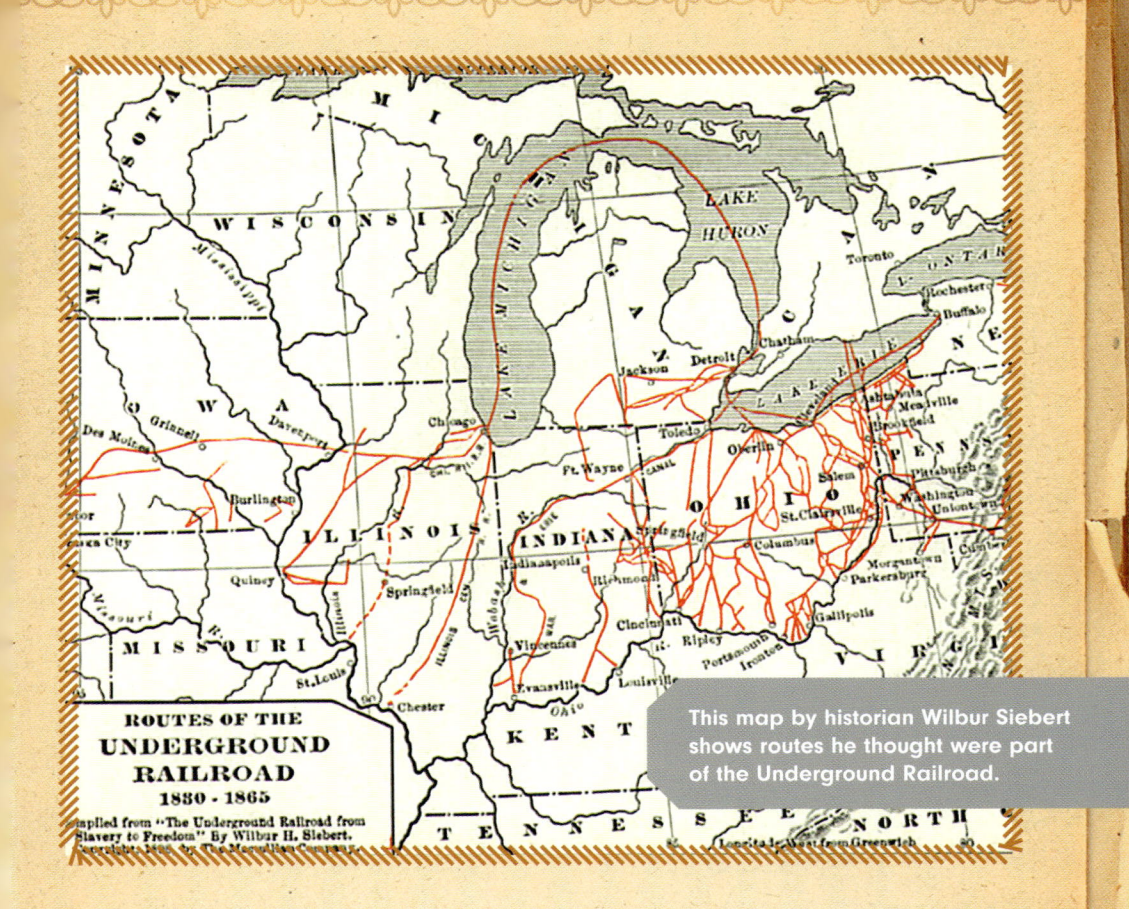

ROUTES OF THE
**UNDERGROUND
RAILROAD**
1830 - 1865

Compiled from "The Underground Railroad from
Slavery to Freedom" By Wilbur H. Siebert.
Copyright 1898, by The Macmillan Company.

This map by historian Wilbur Siebert shows routes he thought were part of the Underground Railroad.

~ Routing the Railroad ~

Many think both **abolitionists** and enslavers **exaggerated** the organization of the Underground Railroad to help their causes. In 1898, historian Wilbur H. Siebert published detailed maps of the supposed routes of the Underground Railroad. Despite this, historians now believe that it wasn't actually so neatly structured. Historian Eric Foner stated that the Underground Railroad was a "series of local networks . . . which together helped a substantial number of fugitives reach safety in the free states and Canada." While most Underground Railroad routes headed north, others led south to Mexico and the Caribbean.

A Risky Escape

Escaping to freedom was a difficult and high-risk task. Escapees left in the middle of the night, sometimes led by a conductor pretending to also be enslaved. They often traveled 10 or 20 miles (16 or 32 km) until they reached a depot where they could rest safely. Then they waited until the next stop could be notified and prepared for them. It was illegal for anyone to help enslaved people in any way once they had escaped, so conductors, stationmasters, and stockholders were all at risk too.

In 1850, the Fugitive Slave Act was passed. It required that all runaways be returned to their enslavers. People who helped the escapees were supposed to be punished. Even formerly enslaved people who had escaped to free states had to be hidden due to the act.

CAUTION!!

COLORED PEOPLE
OF BOSTON, ONE & ALL,

You are hereby respectfully CAUTIONED and advised, to avoid conversing with the

Watchmen and Police Officers of Boston,

For since the recent ORDER OF THE MAYOR & ALDERMEN, they are empowered to act as

KIDNAPPERS
AND
Slave Catchers,

And they have already been actually employed in KIDNAPPING, CATCHING, AND KEEPING SLAVES. Therefore, if you value your LIBERTY, and the *Welfare of the Fugitives* among you, *Shun* them in every possible manner, as so many *HOUNDS* on the track of the most unfortunate of your race.

Keep a Sharp Look Out for KIDNAPPERS, and have TOP EYE open.

APRIL 24, 1851.

This 1851 poster from Boston, Massachusetts, warned of slave catchers. The outdated term "colored people" refers to Black people. Today the term is generally considered offensive.

~ Disguising Runaways ~

Even though the Underground Railroad wasn't a real railroad, sometimes those running away did have to use trains to travel longer distances. They also had to use boats to cross water. When they used these forms of transportation, they couldn't look like they were enslaved. If they did, people would know they were fleeing. Instead, they needed to look like free Black people. This meant wearing clothes that weren't worn or ragged. Both transportation and new clothing cost money. Funds were often donated by generous individuals or raised by antislavery groups.

Conductors and stationmasters were important in helping freedom seekers. Probably the most well-known conductor was Harriet Tubman. She's known to have helped rescue about 70 people from slavery and likely gave instructions to about 70 more who continued to freedom on their own. Tubman told Frederick Douglass, an escaped enslaved man who became a famous abolitionist and writer, that she "never lost a single passenger" on her travels using the Underground Railroad.

Tubman was born into slavery in Maryland around 1820. In 1849, afraid that she would be sold, she

left on foot and walked to Pennsylvania, stopping along the Underground Railroad on the way. The next year, she went back to get her sister and sister's children. On her third trip, she rescued her brother. She wanted to continue helping others escape.

Before becoming a conductor, Tubman used the Underground Railroad for her own escape.

Frederick Douglass (left) said of Harriet Tubman (above), "I know of no one who has willingly encountered more perils and hardships to serve our enslaved people."

~ More About Harriet ~

Harriet Tubman was nicknamed "Moses," after the Hebrew leader in Judaism and Christianity who led his people out of slavery. In addition to her work on the Underground Railroad, Tubman also worked as a **Union** spy during the American Civil War (1861–1865). All those trips back and forth between the North and the South leading people to freedom made her very familiar with the land. She worked with a group of other formerly enslaved people and reported on the movement of the **Confederate** troops, sometimes posing as an enslaved person herself.

Brooklyn's Depot

Many Underground Railroad depots were privately owned homes, but some were public buildings. These depots could be found all over the country. One was the Plymouth Church of the Pilgrims in Brooklyn, New York. An Underground Railroad conductor named Charles B. Ray brought passengers to the Plymouth Church from Manhattan. The freedom seekers probably hid in the basement.

Though it only opened in 1847, the Plymouth Church of the Pilgrims was one of the most important places for the antislavery movement.

The minister of this church was Henry Ward Beecher. He was the brother of the author Harriet Beecher Stowe, who wrote the antislavery novel *Uncle Tom's Cabin*. Beecher was famous himself for his antislavery preaching. Every week about 2,500 people attended Plymouth Church to hear Beecher's sermons, which were also printed and passed around. Beecher encouraged people to resist slavery, disobey the Fugitive Slave Act, and become active in the Underground Railroad.

Henry Ward Beecher is pictured here with his sister, Harriet Beecher Stowe.

~ Brooklyn's "Grand Central Depot" ~

The Plymouth Church of the Pilgrims was known as Brooklyn's "Grand Central Depot" because it sheltered and cared for so many people seeking freedom. A tunnel-like basement below the church hid those on their way to Canada. Not only did the church welcome freedom seekers, but Beecher encouraged his **congregation** to actively participate in and support the Underground Railroad. He wanted people to understand how terrible slavery really was. He occasionally held pretend slave **auctions** in the church to show the cruelty of enslavement.

Board at the Fort

One of the only Union-controlled military buildings in the South during the Civil War was Fort Monroe in Virginia. This military base also played a role in helping some escape slavery.

In 1861, people enslaved by Confederate colonel Charles Mallory were working on Confederate military projects near the fort. They heard they were to be moved to North Carolina, further into Confederate territory. So, on May 23, they sought safety within Fort Monroe. General Benjamin F. Butler refused to send the people back to their enslaver, as the Fugitive Slave Act required. He said they were "**contraband** of war."

In August 1861, Congress passed the Confiscation Act, allowing the Union to confiscate, or take, any property from the Confederates. This meant they could take enslaved people, as they were considered property.

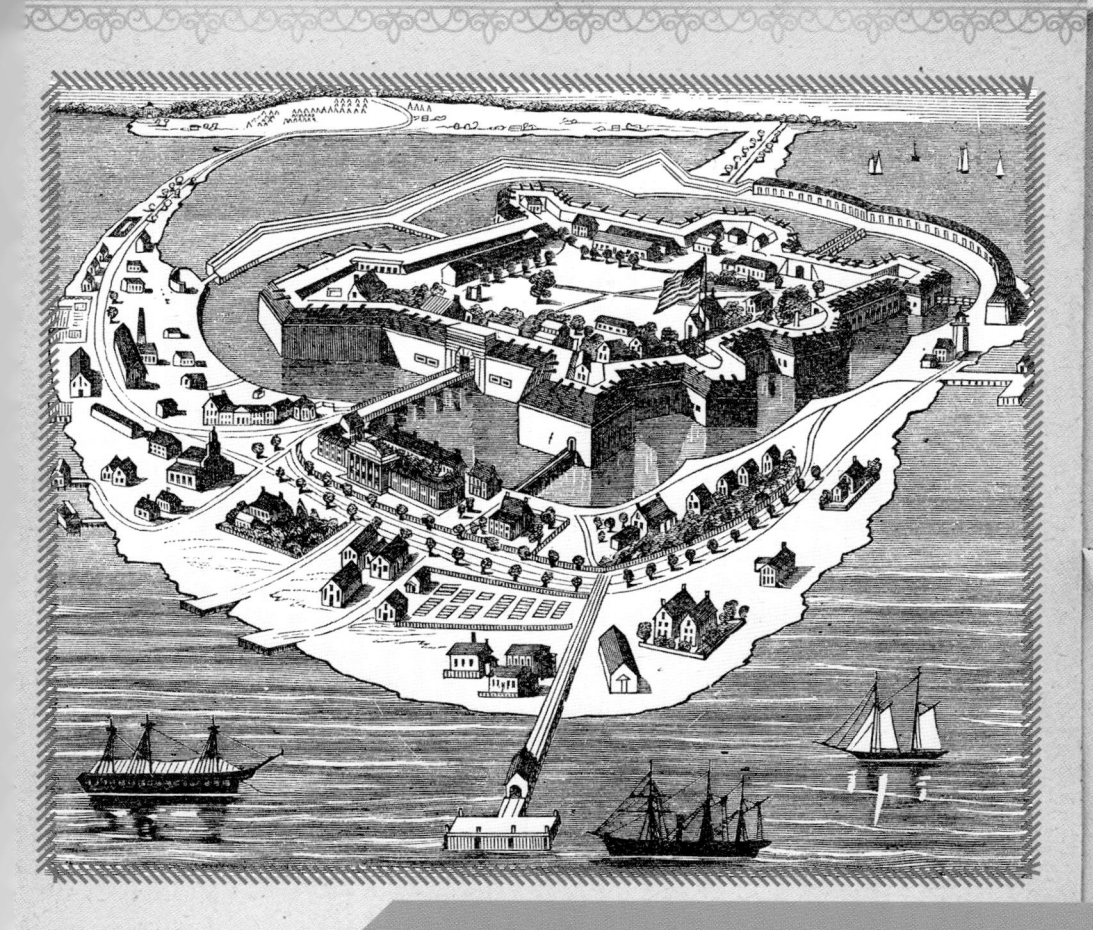

Fort Monroe was sometimes known as the "Freedom Fortress."

~ Life at the Fort ~

Once the Confiscation Act was passed, thousands of freedom seekers began traveling to Fort Monroe. By the time the war ended in 1865, more than 10,000 had come to the fort for safety. The formerly enslaved worked to earn their stay. They completed labor such as building roads. This led some to argue that those who escaped to Fort Monroe weren't actually free at all but had only changed enslavers. Harriet Tubman also worked at Fort Monroe for a time. She worked as a nurse, cooked, and did laundry.

The Thomas House

The first doctor in Kalamazoo County, Michigan, was also a big part of the antislavery movement in the state. His name was Nathan Thomas. His strong antislavery views led him to start a newspaper devoted to antislavery news. Between the years 1840 and 1860, Thomas and his wife Pamela Brown Thomas aided the Underground Railroad. Their home in Michigan was a depot for between 1,000 and 1,500 freedom seekers who were eventually taken to Canada by way of Detroit.

The Thomas House

The couple provided food, mended clothing, and treated the injuries of escapees. Their work was done at night and in secret, but neighbors knew about it and even helped with food. Pamela Brown Thomas's memoirs, or writings about her life, have informed much of what we know about their involvement in the Underground Railroad.

Michigan, being so close to Canada, played an important role in the Underground Railroad. Today, the Gateway to Freedom International Memorial in Detroit reminds visitors of that role.

~ On the Quaker Line ~

The Thomases were Quakers. Escapees who came through the area where the Thomases lived were said to be "on the Quaker Line." This was the nickname for a series of Underground Railroad depots in Michigan. John Cross, a Quaker from Indiana, is thought to have been one of the organizers of the line. He also **recruited** local "conductors" like the Thomases.

Other Quakers helped along the line too. Zachariah Shugart often brought freedom seekers to the Thomas home. Later, Thomas would bring them to another Quaker named Erastus Hussey.

Henderson Lewelling moved to Salem, Iowa, in 1837 with his brother. The two planned to open a general store. Salem was the first Quaker community in the state of Iowa. There, Lewelling helped establish the Abolition Friends Monthly Meeting. This meeting was attended by Quakers who not only opposed slavery, but also wanted to help those seeking freedom from it. In addition to being the home of the monthly Abolition Friends meetings, Lewelling's house was also an Underground Railroad depot, welcoming the formerly enslaved on their journey to freedom.

Hiding places, such as trapdoors, were built into the house. A tunnel under the house connected to a basement fireplace, allowing those who were seeking freedom to slip away easily when people looking for them arrived.

Freedom seekers were often hidden below floorboards with trapdoors such as this one at the Lewelling Quaker Museum.

The Henderson Lewelling House was an important depot that helped many on their journey to freedom. Today it is a museum.

~ *From Missouri to Salem* ~

Salem is only 25 miles (40 km) from Missouri, a state that allowed slavery. A well-known enslaver from Missouri, Ruel Daggs, came to Lewelling's house with armed men and threatened the residents and the entire town of Salem. Still, he was unsuccessful in getting those who had escaped his enslavement back. According to the *Iowa Journal of History and Politics*, Daggs "finally realized the difficulty of holding slaves so near the free State of Iowa and contemplated selling his slaves south so that he would be free from the necessity of keeping a constant guard on valuable property."

Joseph Goodrich's Milton House

Members of another religion that stood passionately against slavery were Seventh Day Baptists. Joseph Goodrich was born in 1800 into a Seventh Day Baptist family in Massachusetts. In 1838, he traveled to Wisconsin with other Seventh Day Baptists and founded the town of Milton. It was located near Rock River, a **tributary** of the Mississippi River—and a route for enslaved people escaping to Canada.

Goodrich built an inn called the Milton House around 1845. The inn was also a refuge for those who had escaped enslavement. To avoid being seen by inn guests, freedom seekers entered a log cabin behind the inn. A trapdoor into the cabin's basement led to a tunnel that ran to the inn's basement. There, Goodrich supplied food and beds for the escaped.

Part of the Milton House is shaped like a hexagon. This means it has six sides.

Part of the original Milton House cabin still stands today. Escapees used a trapdoor inside the cabin to enter the tunnel (left) that led to the basement of the inn.

~ A Crawl to Freedom ~

The tunnel that ran from the Goodrich cabin to the inn was built after the inn was completed. It had been dug into the earth and was only 3 to 5 feet (0.9 to 1.5 m) high. The channel was so small that those using it would have had to crawl on their hands and knees in total darkness for 45 feet (13.7 m) from the basement of the cabin to the basement of the Milton House. In the 1950s, the tunnel was made larger for visitors of the house, which is now a museum.

Gerrit Smith

In 1835, 600 antislavery supporters gathered for a conference at a church in Utica, New York. Abolitionist Gerrit Smith was one of them. A large group of **rioters** stormed the building during this gathering, forcing the meeting to end. Smith offered to host the meeting on his own estate in Peterboro, New York. These events led to Smith serving as the president of the New York Anti-Slavery Society between 1836 and 1839. He encouraged abolitionists to help people escape slavery.

In the 1840s and 1850s, Smith was a stationmaster in the Underground Railroad too. His estate was well

known as a safe place for passengers on their way to Canada. Smith also helped free Black people start lives locally by either giving away or selling land at a low price.

Gerrit Smith, shown here, was cousins with famous women's rights leader Elizabeth Cady Stanton.

The Gerrit Smith House was destroyed by fire in 1936. However, much of the estate remains and can be visited today.

AM I NOT A MAN AND A BROTHER?

~ A Gift of Wealth ~

Gerrit Smith was a generous man, often giving money to abolitionists for expenses. It's estimated that he gave away over $8 million in his lifetime—which in today's money would be more than $1 billion! He sometimes purchased enslaved people directly from their enslavers in order to free them. Some thought he shouldn't give money to enslavers, but rather give it to organizations that fought slavery. Smith also gave money to John Brown, who would raid a weapons storehouse in Harpers Ferry, Virginia, in 1859 in a failed attempt to start a slave rebellion.

Nathan and Mary Johnson

Nathan and Mary "Polly" Johnson made some of the most important contributions to the Underground Railroad in Massachusetts. They were free Black Quakers who lived in New Bedford, Massachusetts. There, they owned a whole block of properties and helped many freedom seekers to escape slavery. The most well-known person they helped was probably abolitionist Frederick Douglass. In fact, the Johnson house was Douglass's first home after he escaped from slavery in 1838.

Frederick Douglass

After Nathan left for the California Gold Rush in 1849, Polly housed at least one more fugitive on their journey to seek freedom from slavery. Polly helped pay for and maintain their properties in New Bedford by selling candy and cakes. Today, the Johnson house is a National Historic Landmark and is owned by the New Bedford Historical Society.

This was the first home Frederick Douglass lived in after escaping enslavement. For safety, those who escaped slavery often changed their names. Nathan Johnson helped Frederick decide on the last name "Douglass."

~ The Community of New Bedford ~

In 1853, New Bedford had a higher population of African Americans than any other city in the Northeast. Almost 30 percent of these residents reported that they had been born in the South. The number of people living there who had escaped from slavery ranged from 300 to 700. Some New Bedford schools and neighborhoods were integrated, which was unusual at that time. Additionally, Massachusetts was one of only five states that allowed Black people to vote at the time. This attracted many free Black people.

More to Learn

The Underground Railroad was a huge effort by many people. This book only names a few of the depots we know about today. It also only mentions some of the brave individuals who risked their lives escaping slavery or helping others do so before slavery was finally abolished in 1865.

Many depots no longer stand, and some probably weren't recorded at all. Their routes and the people who acted as conductors and stationmasters on them remain a secret. But because of these depots and people, thousands of formerly enslaved people found freedom.

Timeline of the Underground Railroad

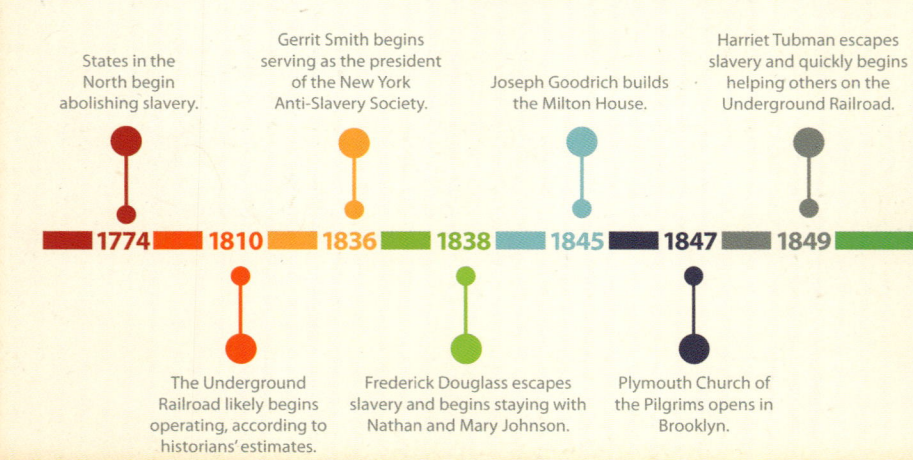

1774 States in the North begin abolishing slavery.

1810 The Underground Railroad likely begins operating, according to historians' estimates.

1836 Gerrit Smith begins serving as the president of the New York Anti-Slavery Society.

1838 Frederick Douglass escapes slavery and begins staying with Nathan and Mary Johnson.

1845 Joseph Goodrich builds the Milton House.

1847 Plymouth Church of the Pilgrims opens in Brooklyn.

1849 Harriet Tubman escapes slavery and quickly begins helping others on the Underground Railroad.

Today, many places that were depots along the Underground Railroad are museums or historic sites. Visiting these places can help you learn much more about this important part of history. Ask an adult to help you find out if one is near where you live.

~ Public Support ~

Some historians estimate that about 100,000 people escaped slavery using the Underground Railroad. Not all abolitionists kept their work with the Underground Railroad so secret. In fact, many were quite public with their views and actions despite the consequences. The governor of New York from 1839 to 1842, William Seward (left), openly supported the Underground Railroad and kept escapees hidden in his basement while serving as a senator. Some northern towns and cities even openly held bake sales to raise money to help the Underground Railroad.

November 1860
Abraham Lincoln is elected president.

May 23, 1861
People enslaved by Confederate colonel Charles Mallory seek safety at Fort Monroe.

January 1863
Lincoln issues the Emancipation Proclamation, which declares all enslaved people in the Confederate states should be freed.

December 1865
The 13th Amendment abolishes slavery.

1850 · 1860 · 1860 · 1861 · 1861 · 1863 · 1865 · 1865

The Fugitive Slave Act is passed.

December 1860
Southern states announce they will secede, or separate, from the United States.

August 1861
Congress passes the Confiscation Act.

April 1865
The Civil War ends.

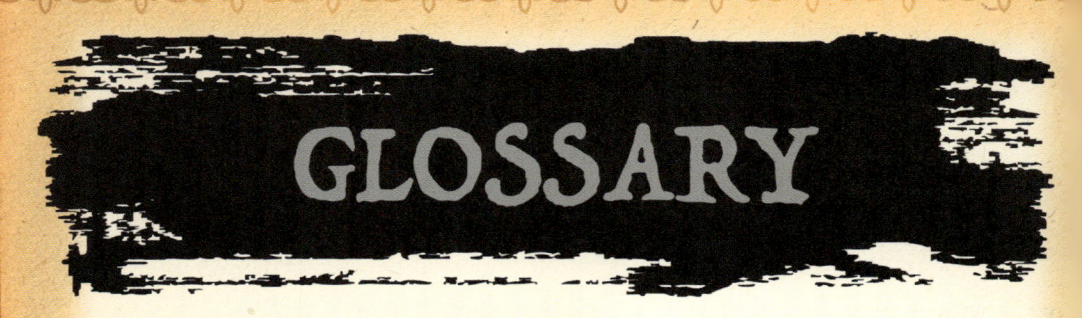

GLOSSARY

abolitionist: one who fought to end slavery

auction: a public sale at which things are sold to people who offer to pay the most

census: the official process of counting the number of things or people and collecting information about them

Confederate: relating to the Confederate States of America, the states that left the United States during the American Civil War

congregation: an assembly or gathering of people, especially for a religious service

contemplate: to think deeply or carefully about

contraband: things that are brought into or out of a country illegally

emancipation: the act of freeing from the restraint, control, or power of another, usually referring to the freeing of enslaved people

exaggerate: to think of or describe something as larger or greater than it really is

integrate: to give races equal membership in something

recruit: to persuade someone to join some activity

rioter: one who behaves in a violent or uncontrolled way

tributary: a stream that flows into a larger stream or river or into a lake

Union: the Northern states during the period of the American Civil War

FOR MORE INFORMATION

Books

Jones-Radgowski, Jehan. *Harriet Tubman*. North Mankato, MN: Pebble, 2020.

Niver, Heather Moore. *Questions and Answers About the Underground Railroad*. New York, NY: PowerKids Press, 2019.

Websites

American Civil War: Underground Railroad
www.ducksters.com/history/civil_war/underground_railroad.php
This website includes links about famous people involved in the Underground Railroad and the Civil War.

Significant Events of the Underground Railroad
www.nps.gov/wori/learn/historyculture/significant-events-of-the-underground-railroad.htm
Find a detailed list of events having to do with the Underground Railroad here.

The Underground Railroad
www.nationalgeographic.org/encyclopedia/underground-railroad/
Read more about the Underground Railroad and find definitions of key terms here.

INDEX